THE BOOK / OR / THE WOODS

We

enter

leaf

by

leaf

Before you start to read this book, take this moment to think about making a donation to punctum books, an independent non-profit press,

@ https://punctumbooks.com/support/

If you're reading the e-book, you can click on the image below to go directly to our donations site. Any amount, no matter the size, is appreciated and will help us to keep our ship of fools afloat. Contributions from dedicated readers will also help us to keep our commons open and to cultivate new work that can't find a welcoming port elsewhere. Our adventure is not possible without your support.

Vive la Open Access.

Fig. 1. Hieronymus Bosch, *Ship of Fools* (1490–1500)

First published in 2021 by punctum books, Earth, Milky Way.
https://punctumbooks.com

ISBN-13: 978-1-953035-51-6 (print)
ISBN-13: 978-1-953035-52-3 (ePDF)

DOI: 10.21983/P3.0308.1.00

LCCN: 2021936384
Library of Congress Cataloging Data is available from the Library of Congress

Book Design: Vincent W.J. van Gerven Oei
Cover photograph: "Forest Lake" by Laisve Ledeikyte, July 15, 2018.

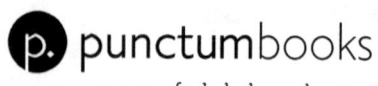

punctumbooks
spontaneous acts of scholarly combustion

HIC SVNT MONSTRA

The Book / Or / The Woods

Jeff T. Johnson

Contents
Of
The Book
Or
The Woods

†††

†††

†††

†††

†††

Preface Entrance : Before & Before

The underworld is everywhere.
—Amanda Yates Garcia, *Initiated*

Part the forest & bare the trees. Make an efes. The Book of books may be a forest of woods, as the page is a clearing, the monster is a letter (for example, Y, who reads the leaves), a river is a mirror, the underworld is supernal, the portal is the shadow over the shades, efes are all about (as wings, as aisles, as the edge of the woods), ††† are trees, The Slough of Decayed Language is near to The Cave that projects itself, or †The Stand of Ob†, shadows fall upon a small shed / larger inside, & ghosts (presence of the dead, who were not dead & are now) sweep every path. All of which are characters. The woods are also a form & a counting, a(n) (in)formal progression : The Book is a profusion of forms that make & remake themselves page by page, for The Woods to exist. Each page an Or. So there is *The Book / Or / The Woods,* and there is a Prologue that appears before & before, & here is a Preface, just as there is, in a collection perhaps to (have) come, *Return to the Woods,* & there may be other stands, for as Jabès & Waldrop say, together & separate(ly), 1 writes 1 book for all 1's time. So 1 may enter here or elsewhere, from there or there, 1 time & another, & 1 is in the woods & also returning. As are we all, whether we are in these woods or another forest altogether.

Preface Entrance : Before & Before

& another thing : this is an epic & ongoing work. We think epic in the sense of bpNichol writing *Martyrology,* Jabès with his books of books, Rosmarie Waldrop's *Curves to the Apple,* Keith Waldrop's *Transcendental Studies,* Harryette Mullen's *Recyclopedia,* Craig Santos Perez's *from unincorporated territory,* Nathaniel Mackey's long song(s), & others. We think epic with these ongoing & collected meta-serial works rather than the traditional notion of the epic as heroic nation building story, though we borrow epic tropes from Dante's supernal underworld forest (& infernal forested underworld), sing with Sappho's lyre, are haunted by the spirit of Homer's katabasis, & are formed by the *Popol Vuh*'s wordly cosmos, which influenced us before we read it. We think/write along with Rachel Zolf, who is composing 1 book in many volumes. We write with friends who are writing 1 book no 1 has yet seen in print. We are in these woods with you & you. We are these woods together. The forest ex-spells us. Here we go again into the lang. The epic is ongoing because we are still reading. Where the forest is our concerns & The Woods is our process & procession, the path we lay down upon as we sink into the leaves.

The Way In & The Way Out

Y the monster is alone in the woods, enclosed by a highway : a preserve. The woods are made of paper; the paper forest burns & burns. Woods & monster are endangered, pressed into service, a hazard. So is the book pressed into service, danger & endangered. The forest is deforested & reforested, dance of shadow & flame, a fantasia of ecological return, the forest (enchanted) by itself. The haunted woods. The ghosts the ghosts of what. This is the world without us. & we are here as well. Here in the forest of language.

The Way In & The Way Out

Y the monster reads the leaves :

Prologue / Earth : 0 The Wanderer
The Book / Water : 8 of Vessels Reversed
Or / Spirit : 16 The Blasted Oak
The Woods / Air : 5 The Ancestor Reversed
Preface / Fire : 6 of Arrows Reversed

The Preface is The Forward in all directions, read before & before. Transition, it reads, a swan ship running back along the under surface of the mirror river. Underworld passage. We begin at the end, wander over blank earth, reflection of the sky, as the leaves show the ††† below. The Book is a moebius loop of water, a stream of words upturned. Or it is all fire in the leaves, a burning passage, spirit of the woods aflame. The Woods belong to the monster, beast of aether, shadow of †††, penultimate letter in the forest of language.

Y the monster reads the leaves :

Origin Story

The Book / Or / The Woods is a serial work that thinks about seriality. It began as the dramatization of a struggle between writer & book, where the book wanted to be an independent entity & the writer wanted to impress a critical & aesthetic agenda on the book. The book wanted to recede from any worldly engagement & be self-contained, but this proved (from the outset, really) to be impossible. Furthermore, it turns out perhaps it was the writer who wanted to hide, in the book or the woods or both. Though the book could not have what it wanted, it still managed to push the writer out of the woods. So the first book, where that conflict played out, was exiled to the end of the collection, & what became the main cycle, the three books named in the title of the collection, took center stage (which is, after all, made of wood, or paper, much like the forest). As for the woods &/or the forest, they are distinct entities, just as they are distinct words, but there is some overlap, & some uncertainty about how they are distinct. Y the monster came to inhabit the woods but was no doubt there all along, an animating spirit, just as the shadows (& shades) were always there. There has been no attempt to make a realistic woods, though the woods are real. Real, but made of paper : much like a book.

The Book / Or / The Woods

All the while, as we were speaking,
We were cutting a path through a forest,
By which I mean a dense forest of shades.
—Dante, *Inferno,* translated by Mary Jo Bang

†b. Of a wood: The edge, margin. Obs.
—eaves (OE efes), *Oxford English Dictionary*

Something is happening.
To the book?
—Lyn Hejinian, *The Beginner,* via Pamela Lu

What about The Woods?
—Corin Tucker via Carrie Brownstein, *Hunger Makes Me a Modern Girl*

The Other Forest

In darkness the scaffolding is foliage.
— Lisa Robertson

The book was a loop
Via *I found myself lost*
In a wood
The book was a loop &c.

The book was made of wood
We gathered in
The leaves this time
Already behind the absent
Line traced in the trees met

Overhead the weaving
Cage are you there
Are you moving
Are you read
Are your hands covered
In text are you listing

Recall the forest from the flames
A floor papered with leaves
The creatures elsewhere
Sentence hung from the canopy
Vines a grammar buffering
The calls of no beast seen

The book or the woods
An archive a selection
The language or the past
No one visits those stacks
You come to on a dare

Ignore the ash at
The efes brushed by ghosts
Translated in the marginal
Moat around the spread

Return to the Slough of Decayed Language

The sentence forgiven the extent to which delayed matter below the boards at one's feet a narrow poison crowding egress to the book splayed with foilage wind blown beneath contemp. A rotting potion of the stand. Leather uppers become the lang. One voice taken by the spring. One voice expelled. The forest aglaze.

A card stuck under a stone :
The forest is what it isn't.

The other, last, former, previous, alternate, lost, decayed, forgotten, to come. The forest. That is, that was, has been, will have become the book.

Rapt in the forest
Taken cover in the book

The book was a forest
The forest never was a book

& yet.

Enter Character Y (A Translation)

Y may enter the forest
But may Y leave?
Not before finding what the forest
Knows.

It is easier to get in
But not that easy
It is easier to get in than
To get out

Return is another matter
But to get out
Is to leave the outer forest
Or to enter the outer forest
From the not-forest

Either way it is easier to get
In though *in 1 place*
Is out another
As Y well knows
But this is not
What the forest knows.

Does the forest know
Y is there
Yes.

Y the character
Knows what the forest
Knows : Y is there
But this is not what
The forest knows
Which Y must know
To leave the forest

Y must not ask
What the forest
Knows the forest
Is the forest of no
Return to the forest
Knows no return
The forest is
As the forest is
Though it must be
Remembered back
Into the forest
After the conflagration
At the end of the book
At the end of the forest
At the efes where ghosts
White as sheets
In a certain light
But covered o'er the impressions
Of leaves Y can see
By the black knife
Cutting away the moon

Y must read the leaves
At the efes where ghosts
Scatter the dust
For none to see.

Silence of the Iambs

So what if Y's foot no longer stirs the dust
Even ghosts at the efes can disturb
& if the cat's claw once entered
Will not retract? 1's life
Is not 1's own
In a forest of devices
Abuzz with agents of oblivion
Not to mention the cat's shadow
Against the wall of trees at the edge
Of the last forest before the end of this word

It may be Error but no accident that leads Y here
In a past brought up to date in a forest papered over in
numbered sheets
Because Y appears in this clearing (papered over as it is,
counted &
Recounted), this impasse is inevitable, until it passes
Into another immutability

If Y circles 1 tree
Y follows Y
Through the forest
Of the tree

That was called

The Forest of the Tree

The forest efes a border
Woven 1 & 1 with trees
See the forest from the efes

They sweep the border
With a hum & exhaust
The ghosts unmanned by selves passed

Count the forest
1 & 1 & 1
The forest of the tree

Enter the Monster

Every forest needs a monster
Whether or not it exists

The monster punctuates the forest
The monster binds the forest

The monster is Y
The forest

What does the monster do? We do not know, as we are (& are) not there, & where is there, & what is there, & the monster blurs the trees, a blur in the trees.

Does the forest make the monster or
Does the monster make itself a forest?
1 cannot see the monster for the trees.

Y the monster character, hybrid pronoun, misshapen punctuation, question absent mark, undecided spot, mouth tuned to the canopy, standing on 1 leg.

O pronominal monster!
Y, lead the way!

Blame

Monster! Ideogram! Beast!
Repeat! Hellmouth! Kickstand!
Slurp! Repeat! Maw!
Crier! Sneak! Repeat!

A sentence follows
The monster
O'er
The wood.

The Monster Read

Y the monster has a deck of cards. The back of each a forest. The monster lays a cross along discarded leaves. The cards are invisible, but the monster knows they are there. A forest covers the forest floor. The cross has a crown & a base, a behind & a before, a stand of 4 leaves at the right. The querent bends over the cross. Dark robe. 4 talents inverted. Justice. 9 cups full. Devil on his head. Horse carries coin. Coin on page. A page, a sword. 10 wands plucked down. 7 grown coins. 10 cups arrayed.

The monster disappears behind a tree.

Who calls out the monster, & whom does the monster hear?
Who reads the scattered leaves that make the forest floor?
The shadows know what they do not tell
The forest hides more than its trees
& what is that shade upon the page?

& where did the monster go
Strikes the question the book refused to pose
Or waves the match the book would not raise
Or lifts the book in question
Then throws it to the efes

The book escapes to the forest
Where the formal shadows gather
& the winds do not appear to blow
The names from the paper

For is the forest in the book
Or is the book on the forest floor
Wrapped in itself, a forest for its cover?

Or the Woods

In a traditional fairy tale there is no need for a portal.
— Kate Bernheimer

Let us hang here (by) the portal : Hereby let us hang the portal O. There is no need to go through, where the other side is at 1's back, & the portal is gone. (O) 1 must keep 1's eye on the portal or the wor(l)d sticks.

O how (does) the portal look(s!)? The portal looks back. O the portal glares in 3:4, ratio bound by false notation, partial obelisk, a sign 1 might exi(s)t (on) both sides at once, all things (un)equal. A gate. A gale.

O the portal is the book in the woods, the woods in the book : (Book : Woods°)

But we have already passed (through) the portal, entered the woods, opened the book, closed ourselves (in).
We (who) were here all along.

° Woods † Book

On either side, as fiction allows, 1 faces the portal. The view is the same. Discard false symbols, where 1 thing leaves the next. Return to the breaks that line the book or the woods. The flickering slash at the forest efes.

1 enters the forest

Or

The forest

1 enters

The book

Or

The woods

1 enters

The efes

What is that sound from the efes?
A roar
Or a hush
Or a scrapèd string?
What grave accent o'er the woods?

& what grave harmonic emerges there?
What invisible disguise?†
What the Sphinx knows
The Sphinx keeps enpawed

Go on from there, emerge
From the road beyond the forest

Through the efes, called by a low tone
Risen from the surface holding up the trees
Here lies the form of 1 held up by an supernal horn

† & what visible guise?

This forest left blank.

for

The forest has no plot.

& yet, a clearing, as though the forest recalls its end. But a

sentence
may
precede
itself &
may
follow
false
paths. Or
what
appears
(to
whom?)
as a path
may be
the
space
between
trees, or
a scar of
leaves.

The
clearing
swaps
the
margin
for the
body, the
copse
along the
frame. It
is as
though
the
leaves
hide a
window
in the
floor,
though
there is

no space below, only the infernal reflection in the leaves.

Remember the monster whose fur is glazed in blood whose teeth are stained whose claws have descended[†] from flesh who loves the dark who knows the blank parts of the forest who shuns the night

[†] whose clause distended

O'er the woods.

Monster, thy name is Y thy face a mask of skin thy forest a coat of leaves thy deck the future past thy floor beneath thy trees O Monster Y in thy forest safe from car commercials & humiliating jobs but not so far removed from efes we cannot hear thy stomach growl.

Already we are in the woods
Which is the most direct route to
We found ourselves (in) the woods
But something there is that doesn't love[†]
The direct route or the familiar line
Though part of us loves that same
Buzz in the foliage, the promise of the hive

[†] a tepid woods

Hidden

Here trees are marks.
— Michael Palmer

Hidden in the woods this whole time, hidden in the woods hidden in the forest, hidden in the paper hidden in the trees. This whole time, this whole forest, this whole woods. Hidden in the book, hidden in the woods. Not Y but W, hidden in the woods. The sound of the wind, the whisper in the woods, W in the woods, hidden in the trees. Her hand on the alarm. Hidden in the woods.

Y hid behind W, after W hid behind Y. Tree before W before Y, after tree before Y before W. W & Y winding around tree, first 1 tree & then the next, 1 tree & 1 tree & 1.

The tree before the tree before the tree.

That a book on paper is a forest is vanishing time is emergent from its own conditions is the superposition of 1 & 1 & 1 tree is a number of numbered pages is written on leaves is the floor on which the forest stands, is Y the monster hidden in the efes.

To the extent the book is every book, the book is every book the book may be.

The forest, though, is no theoretical forest, except in that the world is 1 possible world.

Experience of Y the monster
In space
The woods
Not
Outside the forest
Looking in
Or
Looking out in
The forest
From the efes
Y the monster experiences
Not
Experience of the monster

If the forest is without &
The woods within
& each page a new stand
Each tree in fact a page
The Forest Without &
Call it
The & Of The Woods
There are no small words
But
The woods exist
Whether or not the book
But the forest
The forest needs the trees

A textbook example
Of linguistic alchemy
Or bias
Where what sounds best
Is what is
Whereas
There is
The book

Or

The woods

So

The reverse is true

The woods need

The trees

While

The forest goes on

With or without

The book

&

The book

Eats woods

And shits lit

The & Of The Woods

No

No words

Are small words

The words before the trees

The forest develops a blur
1 cannot read the woods
The capital numbers skew
Toward the efes where
Y the monster lies

The forest
That is
Begins to fade
Or recede

The forest lost
In the trees
Or

The forest
Of woods

Upon us

Nor is the forest made
Of woods

Whether
The forest array the woods
Or the woods make a forest

The book
Or
The woods
But the forest

The blur between
The living & the dead

Crossing (The Obelus, 1 Divided)

The dagger symbol originated from a variant of the obelus (plural: obeli), originally depicted by a plain line (-) or a line with one or two dots (÷). It represented an iron roasting spit, a dart, or the sharp end of a javelin symbolizing the skewering or cutting out of dubious matter.

The obelus is believed to have been invented by the Homeric scholar Zenodotus as one of a system of editorial symbols. They were used to mark questionable or corrupt words or passages in manuscripts of the Homeric epics.

...

[T]he obelus was used for corrective deletions of invalid reconstructions. It was used when non-attested words are reconstructed for the sake of argument only, implying that the author did not believe such a word or word form had ever existed. Some scholars used the obelus and various other critical symbols, in conjunction with a second symbol known as the metobelos ("end of obelus"), variously represented as two vertically arranged dots, a γ-like symbol, a mallet-like symbol, or a diagonal slash (with or without one or two dots). They were used to indicate the end of a marked passage.

— *Wikipedia*

& there is 1
who comes over
but never crosses the efes
except in song
steps over a body
of water & does not
forget the other side

except song lingers in the efes
heard on the side of the forest
if not forgotten in the crossing

Y the monster lays a cross
On the forest floor

Hidden in the leaves
Is the collapsed
Past present future

Y the monster gathers them up
& together they passed behind a †

† The monster split.

Dead Forest

The forest mourns the trees
Says the book
Remember the book
When the water turns to clay
& the 1 who spoke with a horn
Crossed over the woods

The self-same monster
Sleeping by a tree
Adjacent to the 1 who sees

The blind dream
The woods lay down

Their arms in the efes

The Book / **Or** / The Woods

The terrible thing about
ghosts is that we know they are not there.
— Keith Waldrop

The book is
The woods &

The book is in
The woods &

The woods are
In the book

†††

In the book
Is a structure

A small shed
Larger inside

In the book
In the woods

Conflagration

In the shed is a flame, a piece of the larger fire, the light ahead & the light cast back. The shed is in the woods & the woods are in the shed. In the shed, before the flame, is a book.

In the shed of the woods where the monster slept
In the woods where the monster cast its shadow
As space is shadowed place
The shadow of the monster keeps to the shed
As place is packed in space
The shadow & the shed flicker in the light

†††

As the leaves in the trees cast shadows
On the shed & in time the leaves are cast
On the shed & in the shed is the shadow
& the shadow rests in the shed
& the shadow keeps the shed of the woods
& the monster is nowhere seen

An ecology of shadow, tree, pulp, glue & string. The shade & the shed & the shades. The ghosts of woods without the wood of ghosts. The braiding of the efes.

1 enters the forest tied to a tree. The binding is a path along the efes. Tied 1 & 1 & 1. A tapestry. A forest woven on the woods. The efes a backdrop for the noise.

The noise conflates what is inside with what flows. A traffic in the trees. A running in the leaves. The stream goes underground & comes back, as though what descends ascends at once.

In the shed

Is a wood

& that wood

Holds a fire

† † † (Shadows & Trees) † † †

For † say dagger, obelus, cross or t.

† may be the shadow of Y
the monster & †
may be a tree
or the shadow
of a tree
which could explain
why there appear
to be so many
shadows & trees

shadows & trees surround
the shed & shadows &
trees compose the shed
if there were children
in the forest the children would
tell stories about the monster
in the shed the children
would dare each other
enter the shed
but there are no children
& it is said
there is no monster
said by whom

but there is surely
a shadow in the forest
there are any number
of shadows as there are
any number of trees
& there is 1 shed
near the center of the forest
& there is a shadow
over the center of
the forest & there
is a shadow in the vast heart
of the shed surrounded
by shadows & trees

it is said
by whom
there is no monster
it is said by whom
there is only a shed
the shed is shadowed
as the monster is
a shadow over
the character of the monster
which was Y
& is now †
which may be
a number of shadows
& a number of trees

or the shed
may be a shadow
or a monster
or a number of † † †

Book in Shadow, Shadow in Book

The book holds a shadow & the shadow casts the book. The shed holds the shadow & the book. There is a shadow on the shed & a shadow in the vast heart of the shed. The forest holds the shed & the book & the book is a forest & the shed casts a shadow over the book. It is said by whom a book is another & it is said by whom a shadow is another & it is said by whom there is no monster but there is a shadow in the book & there is a book in the shadow & the book casts the shadow & the shadow casts the book.

Intermission

Observers of the forest, the book & the woods (& please note the slippage, though we assure you all is in order & the show will continue), 1 moment as you pause at the rail, dreaming of concessions & the loo, a smoke out front : A point of clarification : The forest has burned, will burn, is burning even now. There is a loop on screen, as there is a loop in the mind, & there is a loop in the breath. We sing the looping fire, the forest beyond repair, the already & to come, the flame & flame & flame. Now, if you please, our time is short.

the stream & the stream

& there is a stream
& the stream runs along the forest
& the stream runs through the forest
& the stream is both the forest

on 1 side of the stream

& the stream is the forest on the other side
& the stream is on either side
& the stream gathers itself
& the stream is current
& the stream murmurs with the shade

on the surface of the forest

& below the stream is a layer of crust
& below the crust is unseen
& unseen there is a river
& the river charges the stream
& the stream murmurs over the river
& the shades fall over the stream

& the monster would drink from the stream &
the shadow of the monster reaches over the stream
& the stream reaches over the forest &
the river under the crust of the forest reaches under the stream
& the shed floats on the river though it appears fixed on the
    forest floor &
cast as it is in shadow
& housing shadow &
shedding shade
& the stream runs through the shed &
the book bloats in the water
& the stream does carry the ashes of the book &
the table made of woods in the shed carries the book
& the table made of woods carries the flame &

the stream runs
it is said
under & over

the forest floor
& the stream
runs the forest

it is said
over & under
& the stream

is the forest
as it runs
back to itself

under & over
what is seen
it is said

& the stream
is a blank
in the forest

& the stream
is a part
of the woods

& the stream
is the center
of the spread

Meanwhile

The forest burns &
Within the forest the shed burns
& within the shed the book
Burns & all is ash & all
Is as it was, as it ever is,
A shed in the shadow of the woods

where
shadow
is
co-present
ghost

The other way
to resurrect the forest
is to turn back
to an early spread
which will soon
bring the fire.

Just so
Y the monster
may emerge
from †shadow
enflamed.

Turn back

Revise

See the ~~forest~~ woods

Before the blaze

Elbows on the very woods
Our Y grew a †
& thereby reinscribed
The forest underneath the trees

†††

Time ceases in the woods
& symbols line up
Along the efes where spirits
Sweep the margins on the world

The dagger
Is a tree

The obsolete
& formal †

Which is to say
The last & former

Obelisk divided
By the cross

Read Forest (The Forest for the Woods)

To read the woods
Is to go in
The shed
Hidden near the center
Of the forest
For the woods
Is the rumor
Of the forest
& the copse
Is a quorum
On the shed

& to walk is to read the forest
& to gaze at 1's shadow on the leaves
is to project 1self
& the surface of the woods
is the screen of the word
supernal

†††

& the shadow is a body below

††††

THIS

††††††††††††††††††††††††††††††
††††††††††††††††††††††††††††††
††††††††††††††††††††††††††††††
††††††††††††††††††††††††††††††
††††††††††††††††††††††††††††††
††††††††††††††††††††††††††††††
††††††††††††††††††††††††††††††
††††††††††††††††††††††††††††††
††††††††††††††††††††††††††††††
††††††††††††††††††††††††††††††
††††††††††††††††††††††††††††††
††††††††††††††††††††††††††††††
††††††††††††††††††††††††††††††
††††††††††††††††††††††††††††††

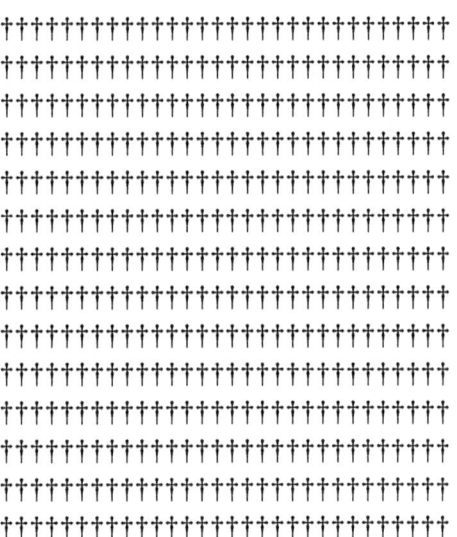

HAS BEEN

††††††††††††††††††††††††††††††

††††††††††††††††††††††††††††††

††††††††††††††††††††††††††††††

††††††††††††††††††††††††††††††

††††††††††††††††††††††††††††††

††††††††††   ††††††††††

††††††††††††††††††††††††††††††

††††††††††††††††††††††††††††††

††††††††††††††††††††††††††††††

††††††††††††††††††††††††††††††

††††††††††††††††††††††††††††††

††††††††††††††††††††††††††††††

††††††††††††††††††††††††††††††

††††††††††††††††††††††††††††††

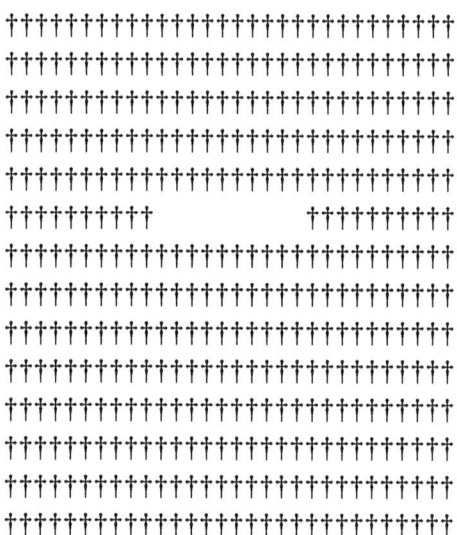

††††††††††††††††††††††††††††††
††††††††††††††††††††††††††††††
††††††††††††††††††††††††††††††
††††††††††††††††††††††††††††††
††††††††††††††††††††††††††††††
††††††††††   ††††††††††
††††††††††   ††††††††††
††††††††††††††††††††††††††††††
††††††††††††††††††††††††††††††
††††††††††††††††††††††††††††††
††††††††††††††††††††††††††††††
††††††††††††††††††††††††††††††
††††††††††††††††††††††††††††††
††††††††††††††††††††††††††††††

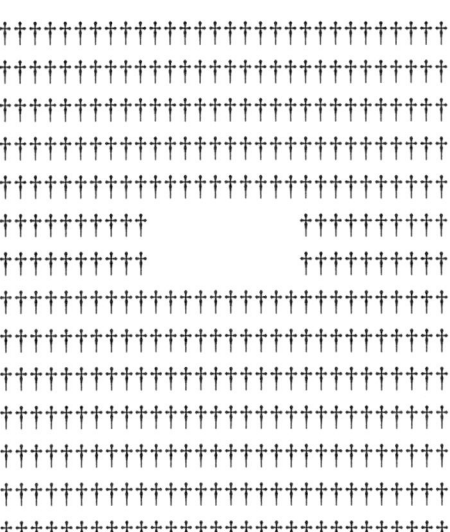

††††††††††††††††††††††††††††††
††††††††††††††††††††††††††††††
††††††††††††††††††††††††††††††
††††††††††††††††††††††††††††††
††††††††††††††††††††††††††††††
††††††††††   ††††††††††
††††††††††   ††††††††††
††††††††††   ††††††††††
††††††††††††††††††††††††††††††
††††††††††††††††††††††††††††††
††††††††††††††††††††††††††††††
††††††††††††††††††††††††††††††
††††††††††††††††††††††††††††††
††††††††††††††††††††††††††††††

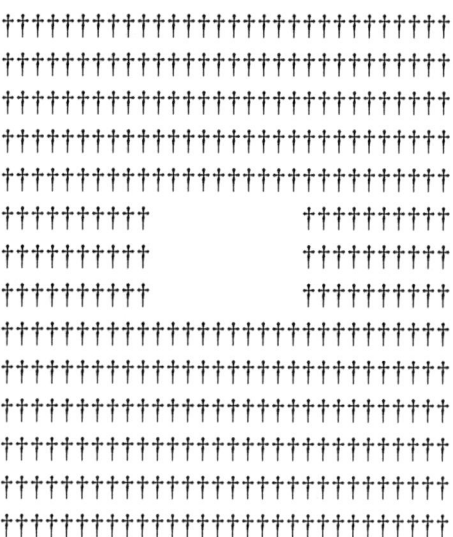

THE BOOK

††††††††††††††††††††††††††††††
††††††††††††††††††††††††††††††
††††††††††††††††††††††††††††††
††††††††††††††††††††††††††††††
††††††††††††††††††††††††††††††
††††††††††   ††††††††††
††††††††††   ††††††††††
††††††††††   ††††††††††
††††††††††   ††††††††††
††††††††††††††††††††††††††††††
††††††††††††††††††††††††††††††
††††††††††††††††††††††††††††††
††††††††††††††††††††††††††††††
††††††††††††††††††††††††††††††

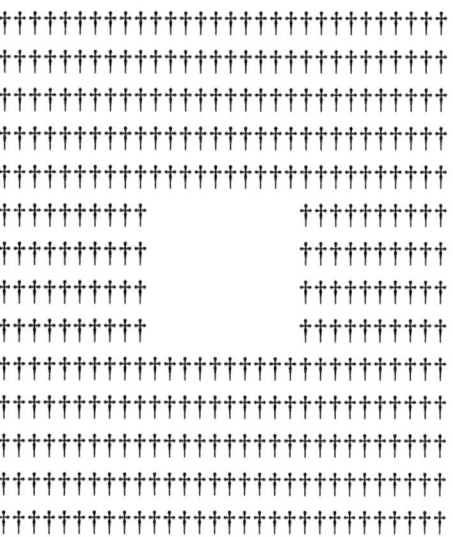

††††††††††††††††††††††††††††††
††††††††††††††††††††††††††††††
††††††††††††††††††††††††††††††
††††††††††††††††††††††††††††††
††††††††   ††††††††
††††††††   ††††††††
††††††††   ††††††††
††††††††   ††††††††
††††††††   ††††††††
††††††††   ††††††††
††††††††††††††††††††††††††††††
††††††††††††††††††††††††††††††
††††††††††††††††††††††††††††††
††††††††††††††††††††††††††††††

††††††††††††††††††††††††††††††
††††††††††††††††††††††††††††††
††††††††††††††††††††††††††††††
††††††   ††††††
††††††   ††††††
††††††   ††††††
††††††   ††††††
††††††   ††††††
††††††   ††††††
††††††   ††††††
††††††   ††††††
††††††††††††††††††††††††††††††
††††††††††††††††††††††††††††††
††††††††††††††††††††††††††††††

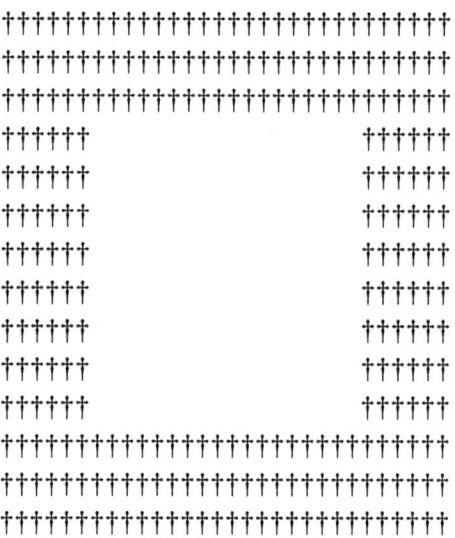

/ OR /

††††††††††††††††††††††††††††††
††††††††††††††††††††††††††††††
††††   ††††
††††   ††††
††††   ††††
††††   ††††
††††   ††††
††††   ††††
††††   ††††
††††   ††††
††††   ††††
††††   ††††
††††††††††††††††††††††††††††††
††††††††††††††††††††††††††††††

††††††††††††††††††††††††††††††
†   †
†   †
†   †
†   †
†   †
†   †
†   †
†   †
†   †
†   †
†   †
†   †
††††††††††††††††††††††††††††††

```
  †† †  ††  †† †  † †††  † †
†
                              †
†                             †
†
                              †

†                             †

†
                              †
†                             †
†
  † ††   †  †† ††† †  †† † † †
```

† † † † †
†
†
†
†
†
†
† †† † †

The Book / Or / The Woods

What have we to fear from the path? Only that we have made it alone.

The Forest Again Revived

In other words, the passageway is an illusion and, like passageways in fairy
tales, it dissolves behind us as we go through it
But then the passageway is no illusion
We are going three ways through it
— Lyn Hejinian

†††

The dark green forest is dark & green for a season. As one season follows the next. The particular bent shadow. Scrawl of branches. Character foliage. Nothing deep enough to lose its way, except that it tries to recover a former path. The forest recovers. Path erased by footsteps. Avenues cut off by trees. Shadows wiped everything.

That was the first forest. The second forest is ablaze. The second forest is red with light. The second forest shines below.

In any space the walls close in. In any forest the door disappears. Shush go the ghosts in the efes. There, there goes the monster into the trees.

But we are already in the trees.

And we are already well acquainted with the monster.

No doubt the monster is something else, as we are something else, as we cannot follow ourselves.

O but our shadows follow us.

The sun at solar noon casts the shadow on which we stand, imagining a surface.

Shadow is not surface. Shadow is something else.

††††

Books pour out of the forest, which empties. The forest has become a factory. The book has become a book among books, a separate thing, one of many. The book does not know the woods from which it came.

The book is both surface & depth, history & circumstance, knowledge of self & emptiness.
The book is the space it takes.

The forest has a book-sized plain that does not correspond with what the book requires.

The book requires a forest in the clearing.

††††††

Shadow is passage, portal of leaves & dust. The portal passes over the infernal world, forest for a cover.

A clearing is a sinking feeling. To the knees. As shadow leads to shade. Layered shadows, endless shades.

Bound up in the book. Efes to crease, to ride the ridge. Forest the supernal version, passage from below.

All this the woods well know
Yet none know the woods

†††††††

The Clearing Forest

Through the woods I'm going / Through the boggy mire.
— Karen Dalton, "Katie Cruel"

††††††††††

There are no woods.
No fire.
The forest is a story.
Nothing in the efes.
The monster
is a shadow.
No sound
in no trees.

††††††††††

To be

In the woods

Is to be

Gone

†††††††††††

a missing page

††††††††††††

So the monster
is in the forest
which is now
the woods.

†††††††††††††

1 †

for

every

  tree

††††††††††††††

The monster
is obsolete.

†††††††††††††††

†The Stand of Ob†

††††††††††††††††††

The †monster passed through the portal long ago, after passing through the trees. But the portal is the ground we walk on. The portal is the shadow over the shades. The portal is the thin shell of the clearing. We have passed there too. To reach the woods 1 must pass through the efes, transcribe the forest, take the stream to the river then step over at the crux.
1 must dilate the stride, leave 1 half behind.

††††††††††††††††††

On the other side is †The Stand of Ob†. We have come to it at last. We who are 1 & 1 & 1. We have become trees, we have become †††. We have gone away.

†††††††††††††††††††

Pity the †monster cannot see us now. And why should the shades not look 1 upon another? For we are shades among shades, all looking away. We have passed through but remain on the surface. Called by a supernal horn. Cast forth by a recent eye. All hands upon the deck : each receives a leaf. To be paired with the hidden card.

†††††††††††††††††††††

The Cast

††††††††††††††††††††††

†

The boatman crosses his fare, whose crossing appears barred. So the floating prison advances, while his staff pierces the crust below the current. He is punching their way through, teasing the surface. 1 is glass & 1 is soot & 1 is hardly there. Staff connects sky, land, vessel, body & bed. All are upended.

††††††††††††††††††††††

††

Fish discovers efes, having crest. All held by the page. The larger body at his back. Flounder become querent, asks to cross. The page is poised. Throw it back.

†††††††††††††††††††††††

†††

Judgment reversed. A supernal horn. Shades below turned up.
Wings turn to shadow. Shortened obelisk. Sky become a crypt.

††††††††††††††††††††††††

The Farther Stand

††††††††††††††††††††††††††††

& who cast the leaves
in the shadow of the stand

& who gathered the deck
from the forest floor

& who lays a cross
on the thin shield of the clearing

& who returns from the darkness
all along the efes

††††††††††††††††††††††††††

For each question answer Y
The †monster disappeared

behind a tree &
appeared on the other side

†††††††††††††††††††††††††††

As what is on 1 side equals
What is on the other side

to the extent what is taken
from 1 is added to the other

††††††††††††††††††††††††††††

what is below equals
what is above

the trees cast
leaves & shadows

at the forest floor
that is the uppermost crust

or the narrow running mirror
that shows the trees their leaves

†††††††††††††††††††††††††††††

Except when there is
a ghost on 1 side
as the efes are ghosted
& the †monster leaves
Y well enough alone

---

††††††††††††††††††††††††††††††††

So that 1 side resembles
another as a shadow
resembles its ghost
or a mirror replaces
what is cast upon it

Mirror Forest

††††††††††††††††††††††††††††††††††††††

of the other side
is reflected on the surface
& what is on 1 side

But ghosts cast no shadows

††††††††††††††††††††††††††††††††††

Or the mirror holds no ghost

& the surface is on 1 side
& the other side is seen through
a forest darkly

††††††††††††††††††††††††††††††††††

for the woods are the story
& the woods are before that
The forest is before the shadow

---

††††††††††††††††††††††††††††††

& the story falls before
the forest & shadows the woods
but the woods hold the story

as the story holds the woods

the woods are the story

So that holding the story

---

††††††††††††††††††††††††††††††

1 enters the forest
as 1 enters the story
but the story is a farther wood

††††††††††††††††††††††††††††

are beyond the story
the woods & the woods
The story though is beyond

---

††††††††††††††††††††††††††

As well the woods
beyond the forest
are a book aflame

††††††††††††††††††††††††††

& light
movement between shadow
Where the fire is

---

††††††††††††††††††††††††††

& the ground is a mirror
through which a shade
passes

†††††††††††††††††††††††

The Forest Leaving

20 pages to get out of the forest
20 pages to the efes
Deck spread at 1's feet
10 turns through the trees

††††††††††††††††††††

You who stand beside the mirror that runs below the trees. Twinned to a shadow. Tied to a †. Whose deck is a book unbound. Whose eyes are flames. Whose maw is an O. The woods recede along the road. A tightening loop. The mirror dries up. Shed collapsed in smoke. Trees plucked 1 & 1 & 1. Shade undone.

The †monster laid bare.

††††††††††††††††††††

For the forest is open & grows more open still. But the forest is a gathering shade. The clearing is a growing darkness. The mirror grows along the forest floor.

The †monster looks down & sees the vast beneath. An infernal sky. The †monster sees the empty woods. The forest for the trees.

††††††††††††††††††

The Cave

†††††††††††††††††

Of course there is a cave
of language
run across on the way
out
	Or 1 might say
there is of course
a woods cast in a cave
we notice only
on our way to the efes

††††††††††††††††

ı may enter
or ı may pass
or ı may already have been in the woods

So that the mouth
of the cave
is the efes

& the darkness in the cave is the shadow
of the woods
fallen upon us

††††††††††††††††

& perhaps then we are gathered here within the book whose walls we cannot see for all the leaves. & as we take our leaves the leaves take us back. The efes are a portal & a mouth & an O. The efes are the final stand of trees. Beyond them lies a forest, the book or the woods. Already the leaves are at 1's back!
& still we ride the †monster's shade!

††††††††††††††

Like the book, the cave produces & reproduces itself, or produces & reproduces the woods. As well they reproduce the means for their consumption. As any book calls its readers into being, &c., & swallows them up. Which includes its so-called writer, its material & its labor. This is not all the cave projects—just as the walls, floor & ceiling are projected, so are the projectors, the cast, the crew, the ghosts & the †monster with their shadows, shades & the very leaves & every tree. Thus we are the contents of the cave. Thus we are the cave. Leaving is as simple as that 1 thing we all do. Simple as the shade.

Retorne to the Sloghe of Langue Decaied

††††††††††

Not all burrowed lang is rot, though ever wood is fungal. Just as the architectonic forest is a metaphor, the metaphorical book is a holomorph. The book itself, grave objet, digital passage. The forest, in fact, is a faux machina.

††††††††††

Ev'ry space is temp, a book w/ ende lef & vygne. Re: space, red agen, resiste tempo tempor. Onely blanc space on the page is < tym. Efen he blande pagne doen mold. An supernal horne ov handgewrit, as upon die lefes & borkr on den forêt dekke.

The ei haf closyd: yon compilated poysyn, the book writes itself.

††††††††

The syntax forged le extant to wheche delayed matter neathe the boardes @1's 2' a narrowe pasion crowing regrette to the book splaid w foilage winde blowed unter contemp. A rotting past of dis stande. Hleder uppe becam the lange. 1 vys tak by sprig. 1 vyce exposed. The forest erased.

Kart be stein impresst :
The woods is where it's at.

††††††

De ofe, layt, frmr, previs, altz, loos, decaed, forgotte, tu comm.
The forest. Tha is, thu was, hab e'en, woll ha becom the book.

Wrapt in the forest
Tk cove un la book

The book war a forest
The forest never wore a book

††††

& yett.

†††

Last Passage

†

The language packt, trees out 1 & 1 & 1. Pensel back in the bo†x. This beene the waye the forest dimns, the woods buryd in the page.

There be fires, there be crossings, there be unmarked decks. There be passage to the foret. There be shadow of the †monster and the trees.

All this book encovered, recompost. For all to passe on light foote. Read as followed, followed as read. Another shadow passing over.

This has been the book or the woods, 1 passed through another. So much for Y the monster, who disappears again behind a †.

The Book / Or / The Woods

The book that comes apart...
— Melissa Buzzeo, *The Devastation*

Words change depending on who speaks them; there is no cure.
— Maggie Nelson, *The Argonauts*

The refrain is the moment when the singer makes it clear that they understand something about what is being lost.
— Juliana Spahr, *That Winter the Wolf Came*

What if I film my way out of here?
— Guy Maddin

We enter the woods
—

Book of Ruins

This is the secret
book that comes before
& after

& is marked
by a dagger
through the heart

of the woods
where Y hides
behind Z

the shield
at the end
& the beginning.

This is the prelude
that comes after
the cycle completed

which is a looping fire
in the woods
hidden in the hidden book

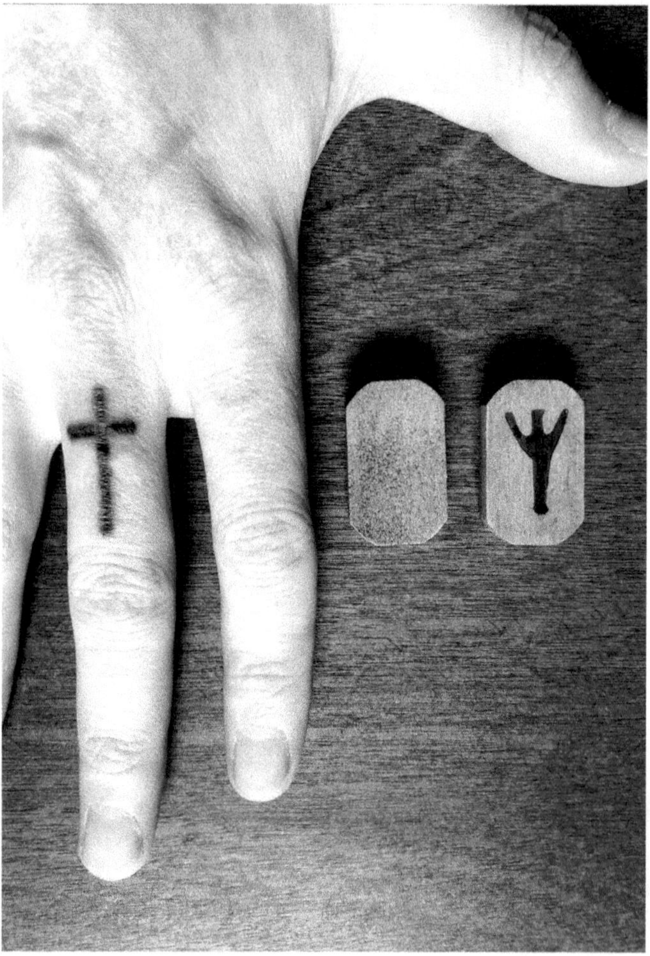

Prologue Preserve

The book should know it's a book as it is written.

Has the book written itself? As any writer has read themselves.

What are the book's concerns? As any writer avoids reading themselves.

In the end of sentences the world was rewritten, not as farce or forecast, not as history but ambience.

The book is preoccupied.

Everything the book says stays with the book.

Let the book speak.

Go ahead swallow the book.

It's already yours. It started without you.

The Book Proper

Here we are then, dancing round content.
The book knows we are here. We open it together.
The book apposed to justice and aesthetic crime.
The book takes what is stolen and returns it to the commons.
The book is a record of its own change.

That the book has written itself does not mean the book has read itself.

The book corrects itself : The book has written but not read itself.

Tired of narrative, the book tried a teratology. The book strayed from the path.

Exhausted by metaphor, the book wrote itself out of the forest. The book betrayed its forecast. The book cast itself. The book foretold.

How long before the plot lost hold? The strong arms of the plot; its vice-like grip.

The plot lost hold. The book run through options. The book is not like a machine.

The book is a machine, but not anymore.

The book remains : a contingency.

For forest read woods.

The Book Returned from an Experimental Passage

No woods is deep.
— The Forest

The book is formed of events, a frame. The book generated in the Capital Regime, amid brutality, in view of atrocity. The book comes from the 20th century & writes itself in the 21st century, as the latter rewrites the former & the former projects the latter. Just so in reverse. The book is the capital of atrocity.

The book is many. A surface. Absorptive. Processed. Forest pixels along the bitmap on an errand. The book stochastic. Turn a corner. Paper over.

The book must be pushed. Just so, the book slid before another. The book pushed away. The book headed off.

Yesterday the book felt heavy. Now it is an empty case.

Contents of book :

Leaves
Ink
Shadow
Diction
Fur
Wood
Margins
Pause
Syntax
Flame

The book contains as well its many versions—what it has been & may be.

The book contained by its grammar.

The book a politics.

The book a rights.

The book means to dismantle a system, reverse the gaze, unmake itself. The book wants to be alone but broods on each device. The book knows this, but can only write itself over & over. The book notices, however, that to write over is something other than to write over & over. Why should this be?

That's the book thinking.

The book is pushed from abstraction; its resting state is form.

This bears repeating. Brutality is repetition & relation — a system, a condition. The resting state of truncheon is holster & skull. The resting state is form.

1 version of the book relates the specific light burden of being 1 Jeff Johnson among many. Of course, every Jeff Johnson is another. Samuel Beckett made this point several times.

Just so, the same person with a different expression is another person. Thus acting & being collapse in character.

This is violence, a form. The confrontation of structure & so-called content, where structure is material concern.

Intertitle

I must forth to my Biz
— Artemus Ward

The book only wants to talk about itself!

This biz about moving the book.

Other territories.

The non-site of the book.

Hidden in detail.

Masked as specific.

What else does the book have to talk about!

The book says : it is false to indicate a general symptom, to condemn an abstraction. The people cannot smash the state. The book plays these little games to keep language in action. The book is problem & process, 3rd person. But really it is process. The book spinning on its wheels. The book is the machine in the machine that makes itself.

Nor does the book care to hear from Jeff Johnson.

Of. Nor does the book care to hear of Jeff Johnson or the shadow of same. The book repeats itself. With a distance.

Repetition with a distance is the title of this section.

Repetition with a Distance

& shadow is enflamed
— The Woods

This section is called difference from the station. The paper leaves. A mark. The book as question.

May a book of poems spoil? Another plot has left its structure, an ascending O. The material wrapping itself. B.K.'s aluminum wall, which surrounds the monster, a wrinkled curve. The monster surrounds itself.

Say the book is the monster enrapt. Say the monster. The book devours the monster as the monster. Absent language gathers around the fire that feeds on pronouns.

The book surrounds itsclf.

Tell

A monster is only or some forest is unseen.
—The Book

The book wants to tell a secret & the secret is listing. If all books were the same design would all books be the same. The book says so. But every book is the same, another book. Beckett again. With a mouthful of Steins.

Rather foliage wipes out cornice, blurs grout.

Indeed it is time for the cat to enter its claw. See it paused over an arm, for we privilege the human.

The pronoun isn't banned, another letter. Survey the craggy text. Reference in the bag, perched as it were along the spine. Language regarded, for the sentence has spread.

Every line comes back as figure, & all that gathers above & below the line is lost, a pity. For there is no line without meeting, as there is no form without reference. Words cover other words, & repetition is a distance. See letters form words but ignore images that lead to a darker path lit by flora.

The shadow of a leave upon the face.

The next page left blank.

Pregnant pause, a gap(e). The book never was a child, no 1's baby, every mother's un-

Pronouns

& shadow is without. & words is last.
— The Sentence

No system or map of tensions : things in flux. The book speaks a language with a tenor. The book does not travel alone. No map but points on a map, foliage the map elides. Pause. Wind through the tries.

Check every passage, head the 3rd way, all hands held down, pointed.

The forest is written on the trees.

The book a record of itself.

For we seek a clearing, if only to set it aside. How else can our selves be seen? Selves who are not clear. Selves to the side.

Irony is cheap but real. The book is an economy. Anything real can be traded; false value defeats reality. A re-placement. The book, reflective object, knows all this & is all unknowing. Every self has a false self, all unknowing.

Therefore we must be clear, to unknow the knowable, to be a world not this one. The book has not become idyllic, but itself. The book can avoid this so long. The book at the foot of the stair, listing.

Last night a version appeared to me.

Every book is a book, some more than others.

Abstraction is its own reward.

Aphorisms are books in themselves, so that a book of aphorisms is properly a library.

Every word processor should have a calorie count.

The U.S. is at war with everything.

What is obvious is worth saying, but cliche has a point : Not everything is worth repeating.

Today a dark shop entered every browser.

4pm Sunday, 19 something else.

Which rhymes with 20 something other.

Tonight is moving night, a double feature.

Back to the trees. You do not know where you are & are therefore outside authenticity. But you own everything. The book does not love or leave you, holds you to the sky, where you bask for a time, apart from the commons, standing among the stands. Copse surround you.

You are banished, then return. Nothing changes.

You are sentenced to write a book.

Confession

A number is dark.
— Jeff Johnson

There are many Jeff Johnsons and there are many many books.
What can we ask of each?

For I have been a maker of zines.

For I have employed the Japanese saddle stitch.

And I have made a perfect-bound journal.

And I have done so again & am not sorry.

For I have composed numerous unpublishable manuscripts.

For I have made open-field digital poems.

And I have sung trouble with the dead.

For I have danced on stage to the Bo Po Manifesto.

And there are books I have read 10 times.

These and other deeds have I done in the name of the book,

As 1 among a legion called Jeff Johnson.

There now go back in the box with all the pronouns hissing each to each around the fire that opens to the night. There is much to leave behind, packed in shadows. There is new foliage on new trees.

The book is an insult to the forest, which hides the book nevertheless.

The book emerges from the forest, drenched in sap.

The book has shed its pronouns, but knows their return.

The book has lost them in the forest. See their eyes among the leaves!

That's Not a Forest, It's a Library

A tree is absent for no forest is silent.
— The Woods

But every book is a changing book. 1 needs only read it once more. Counting again as the Great Figure cast the first stones : 1 & 1 & 1.

The forest is changing too. The forest and the leaves. We — for we are always returning — take our leaves as well. As well we take our leaves. Always coming back as we are.

Here is a chiasmus, a loop, a circular book with a spindle for a spine. The book is ever open and ever closed. That is, open to a different page.

The book is bound to change.

For all the fires in the forest have 1 end : to exhaust. & to purge is man's end. For the fires do not burn at the edge of the forest, or there would be no forest. Or man is the fire at the edge of the forest.

Because this is not a parable, the book must leave the forest. To dwell would populate a symbol, and symbols make sorry scenes.

But, the book asks, have we not left the plot?

But the forest is not a plot.

The Slough of Decayed Language

The leaves without.
— The Book

Not all borrowed language is rotten, though every word is fungal. Just as the actual forest is a metaphor, the actual book is a hologram. The book itself, the made object, a digital artifact. The forest, in fact, is a fax machine.

Every space is temporary space, a book with end pages & spine. To read space, & read again, to resist temporality but temporarily. Only so-called white (blank) space on the so-called (partially blank) page is free of (not from) time. Even the blank page molds. A supernal form of writing, as on the leaves & bark at the forest floor.

The I has it : from a compressed position, the book writes itself.

The Forest Revised

Any text crumbles, … even if we approach the tree before the leaves are falling.
— Rosmarie Waldrop

The language of beasts & the beasts of language may roam that forest, but from its false perimeter their calls cannot be known. The road hewn at this apparent border clogs the ears & clears the mind.

There is in fact no mind.

The book returns to the forest.

Back in the Weeds

A plot surrounded by white space.

of course, the book is a forest
& a cul de sac
world & wald
beast & beat
at best becoming
a copse of words
in margin enframed
the book is no longer
than the 1 sentence
underwritten by a number
of years in a particular foliage
little 1s in a deep bend chasing a loop

O the portal in the grass!

Weeds need landscaping. The forest in the tree. A mold that attends the white space overtaken by letter forms. Written on the forest. Sidewalks through leaves. The whiteness & the witness of streets. The car in the drive.

Sentence to Forget

The book read & forgotten, the book remembered for having been read. The reading a forgetting. Book displaced by its own words. Words no longer in the book. The book of words, but not these words. A way of saying that releases itself, though it is a sentence, which may be suspended o'er the valley.

The book's harmolodic impulse. Each word slides along the register. Unison within and between. Page 85 of every book, or the 85th word of every book in song. Phrases all have equal position in the results that come from the placing & spacing of ideas. The end.

That is 1 end, 1 dream giving way to the next. Artifacts as echoes absent sources. The shape the book becomes.

Forgotten sentence from life's passage.

Each book the book of the dead.

The book would rather be a series of titles, epigraphs, 1-liners. The book would rather be dead. So as not to know what might be said. No, so as not to be in the world. The book its own passage, played out. Thus writerly, no book to intervene. Reader, have at it : Decorate the corpus.

Finale

The end of the book its beginning. The book aflame. The forest alight, come back for it. A conflation.

& now the paper forest has burned, & now the final beams stand, writing in carbon cross the sky, which is unreal.

You who stood with the world before you, who stand now with the world at your back, facing the world again. As though there were a final question rather than a stand of blackened stakes lining the sky, which does not exist.

The sky, which you imagine above the absent forest. The language reels.

Notes : Ghosts

These books & all the others are for Mo & Griff, with love & appreciation for my family.

Thanks to those who read *The Book / Or / The Woods* into existence: Gracie, Willis, Ray, Amina, Claire, Rachel, Julia, & anyone reading this sentence. With gratitude & love for Gina. & the cats: Brix, JoJo, Meadow. Boundless gratitude for Eileen, Vincent, & Dan at punctum, my dream publisher.

Excerpts appeared in *Tarpaulin Sky, Fanzine,* & *blood orange.* Audiobook stream available at punctum audio: https://audio.punctumbooks.com/library/albums/15/

Epigraphs in the Prologue were generated from the following script, adapted from Theo Lutz's *Stochastic Texts,* with thanks to Nick Montfort for his programming class at Babycastles, NYC, & for advice on how to embed this book in this book, a version of versions of The Cave:

```
<!DOCTYPE html PUBLIC “-//W3C//DTD XHTML 1.0
Strict//EN” “http://www.w3.org/TR/xhtml1/DTD/xhtml1-
strict.dtd”>
<html xmlns=”http://www.w3.org/1999/xhtml” xml:lang=”en”
lang=”en”>
<head>
<meta http-equiv=”content-type” content=”text/html;
charset=utf-8” />
<!--
Stochastic Texts reimplementation
copyright (c) 2014 Nick Montfort <nickm@nickm.com>
based on a 1959 program (Stochastische Texte) by Theo Lutz
the text is a translation of Lutz's German text by Helen
MacCormack. Permission to use, copy, modify, and/or
distribute this software for any purpose with or without fee is
hereby granted, provided that the above copyright notice and
this permission notice appear in all copies.
```

```
<style type="text/css">
/* <![CDATA[ */
body {
   background:#000;
   color:#ccc;
   margin:0 0 0 18pt;
   font-family:Optima, sans-serif;
   font-size:16pt;
}
a {
   color:#117;
   text-decoration:none;
}
#main {
   padding-top:18px;
   width:70%;
}
#main div {
   font-weight:bold;
   padding-bottom:9px;
}
#info {
   top:0;
   right:0;
   bottom:0;
   position:absolute;
   height:100%;
   width:25%;
   color:#333;
   background:#999;
   margin-left:6px;
   border-left:thin #000 solid;
   border-bottom:thin #000 solid;
   padding:9px;
   font-size:80%
}
/* ]]> */
```

```
</style>
<script type=”text/javascript”>
var t = 0,
subjects = [‘BOOK’, ‘WOODS’, ‘FOREST’, ‘SHED’, ‘DECK’,
‘MONSTER’, ‘Y’, ‘EFES’, ‘GHOST’, ‘TREES’, ‘TREE’, ‘SHADOW’,
‘LEAVES’, ‘LEAF’, ‘FIRE’, ‘FLAME’, ‘NUMBER’, ‘STREAM’],
predicates = [‘MANY’, ‘SILENT’, ‘VAST’, ‘ONLY’, ‘BURNED’,
‘UNSEEN’, ‘HIDDEN’, ‘OTHER’, ‘FAR’, ‘DEEP’, ‘ENFLAMED’,
‘DARK’, ‘LAST’, ‘FORMER’, ‘NEAR’, ‘DENSE’],
conjunctions = [‘ & ‘, ‘ OR ‘, ‘ FOR ‘, ‘. ‘, ‘. ‘, ‘. ‘, ‘. ‘],
operators = [‘A’, ‘1’, ‘NO’, ‘SOME’, ‘THE’, ‘&’, ‘1&1’];
function rand_range(maximum) {
   “use strict”;
   return Math.floor(Math.random() * (maximum + 1));
}
function choose(array) {
   “use strict”;
   return array[rand_range(array.length - 1)];
}
function phrase() {
   “use strict”;
   var text = choose(operators) + ‘ ‘ + choose(subjects);
   if (text == ‘A EYE’) {
      text = ‘AN EYE’;
   }
   return text + ‘ IS ‘;
}
function litany() {
   “use strict”;
   var last, text, main = document.getElementById(‘main’);
   if (25 > t) {
      t += 1;
   } else {
      main.removeChild(document.getElementById(‘main’).
firstChild);
   }
   last = document.createElement(‘div’);
```

```
   text = phrase() + choose(predicates) +
choose(conjunctions);
   text = text + phrase() + choose(predicates) + “.”;
   last.innerHTML = text;
   main.appendChild(last);
}
function produce_litany() {
   “use strict”;
   litany();
   setInterval(litany, 2000);
}
</script>
   <title>THE BOOK / OR / THE WOODS</title>
</head>
<body onload=”produce_litany();”>
<div id=”info”>
   <h2>THE BOOK / OR / THE WOODS</h2>
   <h3>JEFF T. JOHNSON</h3>
   2016<br />
   ADAPTED FROM<br />
   THEO LUTZ<br />
   <br />
   </div>
<div id=”main”></div>
</body>
</html>
```

We

exit

leave

by

leave

www.ingramcontent.com/pod-product-compliance
Lightning Source LLC
Chambersburg PA
CBHW072040160426
43197CB00014B/2562